SandCastle 2

Baby Animals

D0001421

Calves

Kelly Doudna

ABDO
Publishing Company

Published by SandCastle™, an imprint of ABDO Publishing Company, 4940 Viking Drive, Edina, Minnesota 55435.

Printed in the United States.

Photo credits: Peter Arnold, D. Robert Franz/Corbis, Wolfgang Kaehler/Corbis, Corel, Digital Stock

Library of Congress Cataloging-in-Publication Data

Doudna, Kelly, 1963-
    Calves / Kelly Doudna.
        p.   cm. -- (Baby animals)
    Summary: Simple text and photographs present the
physical characteristics and behavior of calves.
        ISBN 1-57765-186-3
        1. Calves--Juvenile literature. [1. Cows--Infancy.
    2. Animals--Infancy.] I. Title. II. Series: Doudna,
    Kelly, 1963- Baby animals.
    SF197.5.D68   1999
    636.2'07--dc21   98-22060
                                                                    CIP
                                                                    AC

The SandCastle concept, content, and reading method have been reviewed and approved by a national advisory board including literacy specialists, librarians, elementary school teachers, early childhood education professionals, and parents.

Let Us Know

After reading the book, SandCastle would like you to tell us your stories about reading. What is your favorite page? Was there something hard that you needed help with? Share the ups and downs of learning to read. We want to hear from you! To get posted on the Abdo Publishing Company Web site, send us email at:

sandcastle@abdopub.com

About SandCastle™
Nonfiction books for the beginning reader

- Basic concepts of phonics are incorporated with integrated language methods of reading instruction. Most words are short, and phrases, letter sounds, and word sounds are repeated.

- Readability is determined by the number of words in each sentence, the number of characters in each word, and word lists based on curriculum frameworks.

- Full-color photography reinforces word meanings and concepts.

- "Words I Can Read" list at the end of each book teaches basic elements of grammar, helps the reader recognize the words in the text, and builds vocabulary.

- Reading levels are indicated by the number of flags on the castle.

Look for more SandCastle books
in these three reading levels:

Level 1
(one flag)

Level 2
(two flags)

Level 3
(three flags)

Grades Pre-K to K
5 or fewer words per page

Grades K to 1
5 to 10 words per page

Grades 1 to 2
10 to 15 words per page

A young cow is a calf.

Calves live on farms.

Calves are small.

Calves drink a lot
of milk.

This calf stands close
to the cow.

Calves are different colors.

These calves are brown and black.

This calf is white
and brown.

The calf sleeps while its mother watches.

Most calves do not
have brothers and
sisters.

This calf lives with
a horse.

Where do you live?

It is fun to play with
a calf.

Words I Can Read

Nouns

A noun is a person, place, or thing

calf (KAF) pp. 5, 9, 13, 15, 19, 21
cow (KOW) p. 5, 9
horse (HORSS) p. 19
lot (LOT) p. 7
milk (MILK) p. 7
mother (MUHTH-ur) p. 15

Plural Nouns

A plural noun is more than one
person, place, or thing

brothers (BRUHTH-urz) p. 17
calves (KAVZ) pp. 5, 7, 11, 17
colors (KUHL-urz) p. 11
farms (FARMZ) p. 5
sisters (SISS-turz) p. 17

Verbs

A verb is an action or being word

are (AR) pp. 7, 11
do (DOO) pp. 17, 19

drink (DRINGK) p. 7
have (HAV) p. 17
is (IZ) pp. 5, 13, 21
live (LIV) pp. 5, 19
lives (LIVZ) p. 19
play (PLAY) p. 21
sleeps (SLEEPSS) p. 15
stands (STANDZ) p. 9
watches (WOCH-ez) p. 15

Adjectives

An adjective describes something

black (BLAK) p. 11
brown (BROWN) pp. 11, 13
different (DIF-ur-ent) p. 11
fun (FUHN) p. 21
most (MOHST) p. 17
small (SMAWL) p. 7
white (WITE) p.13
young (YUHNG) p. 5

Sight Words

farm

milk

horse